An Oar for Odysseus

An Oar for Odysseus

Poems by

Robert Cooperman

© 2025 Robert Cooperman. All rights reserved.
This material may not be reproduced in any form, published,
reprinted, recorded, performed, broadcast,
rewritten or redistributed without
the explicit permission of Robert Cooperman.
All such actions are strictly prohibited by law.

Cover design by Shay Culligan
Cover image by Gene McCormick

ISBN: 979-8-90146-705-3

Kelsay Books
502 South 1040 East, A-119
American Fork, Utah 84003
Kelsaybooks.com

For Michael, who gave me the title

And as always and with great joy and love,

For Beth

Acknowledgments

The author wishes to thank the editors of the following journals in which the poems listed below first appeared or are forthcoming:

Creativity Webzine: "Odysseus Takes His Place in Hades"

Kronos Journal: "Odysseus in an Inland Village"

Mad Blood Poets: "Klax, the Headman of the Steppe Village, Considers Odysseus and His Two Companions," "Axia Performs the Funeral Rites for Odysseus,"

The Raven's Perch: "Telemachus Watches His Father Leave Ithaca a Second Time," "Tembla, Wife of Telemachus," "As Penelope Walks the Shore of Ithaca, Some Flotsam Washes Up," "Penelope Thinks of Polynides," "Polynides Considers Odysseus and Telemachus," "Odysseus Prepares for Polynides"

Contents

PART ONE: TELEMACHUS OF ITHACA

Telemachus Watches His Father Leave Ithaca a Second Time	15
Tembla, Wife of Telemachus	17
As Penelope Walks the Shore of Ithaca, Some Flotsam Washes Up	18
Telemachus Sees the Skiff in Which He Banished His Father Odysseus Drift Back to Ithaca	20
Eumaios the Swineherd Ponders Telemachus	22
Eumaios Sees the Skiff	24
Telemachus, After Banishing His Father Odysseus, Considers His Subjects	25
Telemachus Speaks to His Mother, Penelope	26
Penelope Speaks with Telemachus	28
Penelope Considers Odysseus	29
Polynides Considers Telemachus and Odysseus	30
Penelope Thinks of Polynides	32

PART TWO: POLYNIDES

Polynides, on the Sea, Searching for News of Odysseus	37
Polynides Compares Himself to Odysseus	38

PART THREE: AN ISLAND REFUGE

Odysseus Finds an Island	43
Odysseus Assesses Their Island Haven to Axia and Miletes	45
Odysseus on the Island	46
On Their Island Refuge, Axia Contemplates Odysseus	47
Miletes Thinks of His Mother and Odysseus	49

Odysseus Thinks of Axia	50
Axia Thinks Further About Odysseus	52
Axia, While Odysseus Takes Her Son Miletes on His First Hunt	53
Odysseus Takes Miletes on His First Hunt	54
Odysseus Compares This Hunt with Those When He Was a Young Prince on Ithaca	56
Odysseus Thinks of Miletes and His Son Telemachus	58
Axia, When Odysseus and Miletes Return from His First Hunt	60
Miletes, After His First Hunt	62
Miletes, from His Island Pine Crow's Nest	64

PART FOUR: SHIPS

Odysseus Sees Ships	67
Odysseus Prepares for Polynides	69
Polynides Meets with Odysseus	71
Axia and Miletes Hide in a Cave	72
While Polynides Tries to Convince Odysseus to Return to Ithaca, the Old Warrior Plots	74
After Sharing a Meal with Polynides, Odysseus Speaks First	76
Kallanx, One of Polynides' Guards, Around Odysseus' Campfire	78
Rhenon, the Second Guard Accompanying Polynides to the Camp of Odysseus	79
Polynides, After Odysseus Refuses to Return to Ithaca	80
As He Follows Polynides Back to the Envoy's Ships, Odysseus Sees More Dilemmas	82
Polynides Makes a Fateful Decision	84
Boreas, Head of Polynides' Men	86
Neseis, "Son" of the Ambassador Polynides	88
Before Sailing Back to Ithaca, Boreas Consults with Odysseus	90
Odysseus, After Boreas Sails Back to Ithaca	92

From Their Cave Hideout, Axia and Miletes Watch the
   Ships Depart   94

PART FIVE: ON ITHACA

On Ithaca, Telemachus Frets	99
Boreas and Young Neseis Report to King Telemachus	100
What Penelope Whispered to Telemachus	102
Penelope Thinks of Odysseus	104

PART SIX: AN OAR FOR ODYSSEUS

Odysseus and His Two Companions Make Landfall and Start to Trek Inland	109
Trekking Inland, Odysseus and His Companions Are Accosted by Thieves	110
Axia, Miletes, and Odysseus Find a Village Haven	112
Odysseus, in an Inland Village	114
Miletes in the Village	116
Klax, the Headman of the Steppe Village, Considers Odysseus and His Two Companions	118
Odysseus Lies Dying	120
Axia Performs the Funeral Rites for Odysseus	122

EPILOGUE

Odysseus Takes His Place in Hades	127

PART ONE:

TELEMACHUS OF ITHACA

Telemachus Watches His Father Leave Ithaca a Second Time

I've no memory of Father's first leaving,
though I'm told Mother held me in her arms
and wept as his flagship carved the waves.

Twenty years later, I've ordered him gone,
tired of his playing the raging Minotaur,
blaming Troy and the sea for his tantrums
fueled by urns of wine; he threatened all
in his howling path, tormented by his Furies,
then wept more tears than the sacks he swilled,
then howled over the little boy he slew
when he and the others burst from the Horse,
as if one small life mattered when weighed against
the scores, hundreds, thousands of dead foemen.

So I hired two thugs to escort him into exile,
and ensure he'd not return. It had to be done:
his drunken disruptions more violent
than when Poseidon sends sea-driven blizzards.
Besides, it's my time to rule, not that drunk
old man, who bored me with the retelling
of his adventures, evening after evening.

Before Mother withdrew to a mountain hovel
on Ithaca's far side, she hissed in my ear,

"Far better men than those two have tried
to send great Odysseus to Hades. Sleep
with one eye open and a drawn dagger."

I scoffed, but felt a chill. In my chamber,
I ordered my servant to build up the fire.

"But my Lord, it's summer," he whined,
then cringed at the murder in my eye.
Father's besotted ravings gave underlings
license to forget who their master is.

Tembla, Wife of Telemachus

As the god-tormented old man was rowed away,
my husband spat, "Good riddance!" Though to me,
Odysseus was never a frightful Charybdis,
but ever courteous, while my husband demanded
more than the Wanderer could ever give him
in the way of a father's love: his years away
from Ithaca shattered the bond that should've
bound them like caressing tree limbs.

As for our tiny Anticles, Telemachus feared
Odysseus would fly into one of his rages and smash
my darling against a palace wall, as I've no doubt
he did to Trojan babies he and the other warriors
tore from wailing mothers—what all mothers fear
in our harsh world of raid or be raided.
But to my son, he was the smiling grandpapa,
bouncing our boy to sleep when no one else could.

Still, Odysseus was never without a wine sack:
the guilt of the men he'd slain made him try
to drown in liquid oblivion, plus his grief
for his shipmates, all dead at Ilium or on the sea,
and worst, the tiny lad he thoughtlessly slew:
his nightly howls of anguish startling the palace awake.

But now Odysseus has been taken into exile
by my husband's assassins, no intention
of delivering him to an island sanctuary.
They'll kill and dump him out of sight of land,
my husband too squeamish of the Furies' retribution
to perpetrate the filthy deed himself.

I wish I'd known the old man in his prime!

As Penelope Walks the Shore of Ithaca, Some Flotsam Washes Up

Advancing and ebbing in the tide,
the battered skiff of those thugs my son hired.
Odysseus sensed their plans when he stepped
on board for his banishment, and I feared
I'd never see him again, not that our reunion
had been joyous: him still fighting the war
and the monsters he so shuddered to recall,

he was never without his wine sack,
too addled to be a husband to me,
a father to angry Telemachus:
Odysseus showing him none of the affection
our son expected, the man returning to Ithaca
a foaming stranger with Odysseus' aged face.

When I tried to accompany him into banishment
and probable death at the hands of these harbor rats,
he and my son restrained me, and in truth,
I didn't fight too hard, so weary of enduring
my husband's endless rages and tears.

Now, I pace the strand, stare at the ruined craft,
and scan the sea, sometimes see a swimmer
breasting the waves, but only a dolphin.
And if my man did return, who's to say
he'd be healed, or the same raving monster
as the one I almost wouldn't mind seeing
washed up on our shore, without eyes, half-eaten.

Telemachus Sees the Skiff in Which He Banished His Father Odysseus Drift Back to Ithaca

Its return? Those two sea rats I dispatched
to kill Father are dead, maybe Father too,
this skiff piloted to shore by his ghost,
to haunt my nights for being an unnatural son
without the courage to kill him myself.
He returned from Troy and the sea a wraith,
not the hero Mother told me of nightly.
He wandered the palace, drowned in wine,
cursing all who dared cross his path,
until no one could bear him any longer.

Even more of a sword flat slapping my face:
what if Father's alive and crazed for vengeance,
biding his time, to let me fret with terror
that he's hiding in my palace, waiting
until my guard's down before killing me
slowly, slowly, like a master torturer?

What if he taunts me with brief appearances,
let's me think he's a spirit, then vanishes,
to reappear again and again, to drive me as mad
as he became: jabbering about one little boy
he slew the night he and the others burst
from the Horse, to leave Troy a smoking ruin?

The worst part? I can't let my servants, vassals,
my wife or mother catch sight of my terror,
nor neglect the running of my kingdom.
So I gather my strength each dawn and pretend
all is as it should be: my husbandry whirring
like the loom Mother put off the Suitors with.

Now, I see they were far less a plague of locusts
than Father was: he's made me dread I'm king,
alive only insofar as I wait to die.

Eumaios the Swineherd Ponders Telemachus

Not possible, with all of his armed guards,
but I long to sink my blade into my Lord's
unnatural son, for sending my King away
with two murderers. Odysseus returned
from Troy and the sea horrors a broken toy:

not in body, for he defeated the Suitors,
as if shooting arrows into frozen targets,
but crushed by the deaths he dealt and witnessed.

Those corpses like boulders forever rolling
over him, as if Sisyphus in grim Hades,
driving Odysseus to howl and moan
through the palace, to futilely beg priests
to lift the curse. So he swilled wine, threatened
everyone, even me, his oldest companion;
even worse, his faithful wife, Penelope,
then when he recovered, begged forgiveness,
only to froth and rage all over again.

And from the way she glared arrows at him,
obvious even to me she'd rather
see him on a pyre than take him to bed.

Still, Odysseus was owed his son's respect,
no matter that Telemachus was primed
to rule, after years of threats from the Suitors.

So I fight my rage whenever I think,
"This puling whelp, this craven, cringing traitor
demands to be seen as our lawful king?"

He's lucky me and the other keepers
of his herds and flocks don't set a trap
for the usurper, the coward, the thief,
and leave his traitorous carcass for the wolves.

Eumaios Sees the Skiff

I feared our King's banishment would end with
a dagger in his back, food for the sharks,
and those two vermin with a fat reward
from his son, Telemachus too fearful
of the Furies' vengeance for kin killing
to carry out the dirty slaughter himself.

But now this empty skiff rises and falls
on the stony strand with each lapping wave;
maybe haunted by Odysseus' ghost,
or my Lord managed to overpower
or trick those two sea rats and drifted back,
to take just revenge on his scummy son,

though something forewarns me I'll never see
my King again, that if he did defeat
and send those two stink-fish to the bottom,
he's declared good riddance to Ithaca.

Queen Penelope often walks the strand,
and when she came upon this skiff, she sought
my hovel, and demanded if I'd seen
my Lord hiding anywhere on our island,
her eyes full of fear that he might return.

I told her no, didn't mention I hoped
he'd rain terror on his shit of a son.

Telemachus, After Banishing His Father Odysseus, Considers His Subjects

It had to be done, Father dangerous
as a blizzard blowing straight down from Thrace:
Everyone on Ithaca knew he roamed
the island besotted as whirling-mad
Scylla, or like monster-Charybdis snatching
mariners like succulent grapes and figs.

Yet all I see are glares hard and freezing
as the eyes of the Gorgon, Medusa:
from the keepers of my herds, swine, and flocks,
the cultivators of my fields and vineyards;
to my house slaves muttering that I had,

"Our rightful king banished and foully slain."

Rightful? How many thought his drunken stumbling,
and roaring fisticuffs were the stuff of
a rightful king when he accosted them,
his breath stinking of wine, their faces bloodied?
They just object to how I disposed of him
with two sea vermin I'd paid to ensure
he'd not plague my kingdom and people again.

Let those who didn't have to suffer his shouts,
to reel from his wolf breath on their faces,
feel the slap of his palm, hard as a sword-flat,
for the offense of begging him to please, please,
for just one night, be quiet—let them swear
they wouldn't have acted just as I did.

Telemachus Speaks to His Mother, Penelope

If I could take it back, Mother, I'd still
have banished Father: daft and deadly
from the War, the sea horrors he witnessed
in strange, perilous lands, and most of all,
his guilt for slaughtering that harmless boy
the night Troy finally fell to us Greeks.

I see the stone glares of my countrymen
who never knew him, but claim they love him,
despite returning with a thirst so burning,
his every swig poured flames onto his despair.

You'll accuse I shouldn't have sent him away
companioned by two murderous sea scum:
to you, I'm a son wicked as Medea
was a mother, but he menaced everyone,
then drowned in tears and begged forgiveness,
for his rages, only to roar again, a maddened lion.

Even you, Mother, could no longer abide
his threats, his punches, his moods terrible
as the myriad-clawed monster, Typhon
when he bursts forth from fiery Mount Etna.

This island unrest will pass; in the meantime,
I'll perform my duties diligently
until my subjects forget there ever
was a king of Ithaca named Odysseus.

Penelope Speaks with Telemachus

My son, you ignored me and justified
exiling your father: his rampages
a disruption to the quiet you crave
far more than the greatness that once berobed
Odysseus like the finest breastplate.
But that was ever your way, even as
a small boy: to assert you knew better
than all the world, especially your mother.

But now, you find yourself treed like a lynx
by baying hounds, and need my wise advice.
So here it is: Yes, let the people see
how well you rule. But also, send swift ships
to seek Odysseus. Alive? Save him
from those brigands you sent him away with,
keep him tranquil with a poppy tincture,
parade him on feast days or when the people
get restless that their lives aren't easeful
as the blessed gods on Mount Olympus.

If he's dead? Drag those vermin back, have them
executed in public, to avenge
your poor, dear, grief-and-drink-crazed father.
On second thought, it might be preferable
if he's found dead, and permanently
kept from returning to make more trouble.

Penelope Considers Odysseus

Husband, you've most likely been daggered
by the wharf rats our son banished you with.
So since you're probably shark food, I gave
our son the pragmatic advice you might've,
to keep our boy—all I have left—alive:
Placate the allies and herdsmen who loved you
before you left for Troy and fought beside you
when you returned. If our son sends search ships,
Eumaios and the others might be softened,
especially if, as I doubt, you're alive.
And if the searchers drag back those sea scum
for punishment, that will go a long way
to proving our son-king's sincerity.

Though I begged to accompany you into exile—
even suspecting your death, and therefore mine,
was what our son planned, or at least hoped for—
let's be honest, every day you roamed the island
upon your much delayed return from Troy
and the sea, you sucked on your wine sack like a teat,
thus less and less Odysseus, who'd won
my heart, valued my sagacious council;
and more and more, a tormented monster
that would topple off a steep cliff, and drag
the kingdom into your own Tartarus.

So, my sad darling, you had to be sacrificed.

Polynides Considers Telemachus and Odysseus

I'd hoped he and his brute-father would kill
each other, thus leave the path clear for me
to wed the Queen, and who knows what mishap
might free me to take a young, nubile wife.
But now that Telemachus has banished
his battle-hard sire, the whelp's exposed:
the old man the only one who could string
the great bow that slaughtered all the Suitors,
and despite his frothing like a mad bear
the Kingdom's commoners worshipped the souse.

So Telemachus has lost a fighting arm
and the goodwill of those who should have been
his fiercest allies; thus fig-ripe to fall,
except he's ordered me to search out
and bring Odysseus home, to assuage
the imp's fear of the Furies. And if dead,
to find and kill the two wharf scum he hired
to make sure his father never returned,
so he's outflanked me, or Penelope has.

I'll make sure we'll never find the old coot
or those two drunken, murderous vermin;
if we do, I'll have the old man dispatched
and claim those sea-rats were responsible,
and that I had them executed right there.

More important, we'll raid fat coastal cities
and sail back with honors and glory enough
to make the island forget our late king,
who returned to Ithaca an old beggar,
guilt-mad for slaughtering that tiny boy.

I'd have slain that brat too, but I'd not
tell the tale over and over, as if driven
by a stinging gnat sent by Father Zeus.
A hero forgets the lives he snuffs out.
What better way to show love of the gods.

Penelope Thinks of Polynides

Do you think I can't see what you're plotting?
Why do you think my son sent you on
this vain search for Odysseus? I whispered
that you were the right man for the errand.

Yes, Telemachus should not have exiled
his father with murderous companions.
Still, he's my son, and I'd rather he rule
than you, sly Polynides, who intended
to wed me, then have my boy and me slain.

But I've advised my son, if Ithaca
is to avoid the Furies, we must send
search parties for Odysseus, though I've
little hope he's alive, and if he is,
hardly fit to return, rule, and love me.
Still, we must do all we can to placate
our subjects, and the gods who rule this world.

Besides, two can play your game, for who knows
what perils lurk at sea or in cities
you'll think are fat, helpless capons, but might
harbor monsters, and if you find my husband,
he's still not a man to be trifled with,
defeating over one hundred Suitors.
Do you think your few crewmen can stand
against him, who has dealt death all his life?

Maybe a second slaughter will purge him
of the curse flung by the boy he butchered
when Troy and the great house of Priam fell.
Maybe not, but if he slays you, enough.

PART TWO:

POLYNIDES

Polynides, on the Sea, Searching for News of Odysseus

I picked men expert at arms, men who can
keep their mouths shut if something should befall
Odysseus, if he's still in this world
and by some miracle, we do find him,
then send him where he can't bother anyone.

I'll wear a face contrite as Father Zeus's
when His lightning bolts sizzle an innocent,
when I tell Telemachus and his mother
that we searched and searched, royal mother and son
winking inwardly, knowing what I did,
and how it was necessary, but also
necessary to keep up the fiction
I, and they, did everything possible
to try to retrieve the guilt-crazed old man.

If Telemachus showed more spine after
ordering his mad father's banishment
I'd not be sent on this foolish errand,
but the brat feared the kin-avenging Furies,
for his hiring those murderous wine-soaks.

And I can claim I made every effort
to find Odysseus, while I foment
the other nobles and lower orders
that Telemachus and his scheming dam
were wrong in the gods' eyes, to banish him.

Polynides Compares Himself to Odysseus

Odysseus' feigned madness failed to save
him from being dragged off to Troy, but I hid.
The harbor all shouting and ship loading,
and in the chaos of preparations
I was forgotten, and escaped the war
and the even worse years on the monster-
and witch-perilous sea.

                        I became rich,
and had the further good sense to avoid
joining the Suitors, since I'd sent out scouts,
who informed me Odysseus was spied
on one island, then another, so surely
getting closer and closer to Ithaca,
and that he'd exact a retribution
so terrible, none of those swaggerers
who thought with their cocks and bellies would live.

And wasn't I right? The Suitors slaughtered
by his arrows and sword, with the aid of
his son and some servants who'd stayed loyal
to him all those years of his wandering

But now he's been banished by that same son,
for his rampaging about Ithaca,
a man touched by the mad-making finger
of Zeus, all for the guilt he can't shake off.

Stupid, to feel crushed by so much remorse
for a child no one will miss, so many
more important concerns to consider,
like my wedding Penelope and slaying
Telemachus, more puling whelp than king.

PART THREE:

AN ISLAND REFUGE

Odysseus Finds an Island

Axia, her small son Miletes, and I
have sailed from Troy, where I discovered her
grievously hurt and stanched her many wounds,
she and her son fetching up after drifting
for days, their village destroyed by marauders,
And me? Returning to Troy, desperate
to remove the curse plaguing me for years.

I've sworn to keep them safe, the only kin
I care to acknowledge, now that my son
has tried to have me killed by the two thugs
he sent with me into what was supposed
to be a soft banishment where I couldn't
disrupt his prudent rule of Ithaca
with my drunken, guilt-enflamed rampages.
And Penelope? She put on a show
of wishing to leave with me, but she knew
my fate, and didn't want to share it: worse
for a woman, before merciful death.

When we sailed from Troy, I took as many
weapons as would fit in our skiff, to wield against
any raiders, or if my son found us
and thought to drag me back to Ithaca:
guilty he'd banished his drink-mad Papa,
or to make sure he'd finished me for good.

I'll hide these, set traps for any attackers,
and teach Miletes the necessary skills
in this world of slaughter or be slaughtered,

though I pray we'll never have to employ
these arms or my deadly knowledge.

But best to be ready than just to pray.

Odysseus Assesses Their Island Haven to Axia and Miletes

From a sail around the perimeter
then a search on foot, there's nothing to fear:
no monsters, cannibals, giants, or witches—
like the ones I pissed myself to escape
while my men and I blundered from horrors
I failed to bring them safely home from.

Just an island, so far off the trade routes,
no raiders will find it, let alone beach
their wolf-ships, bristling with plunder and rape.
The island abounds with game, and the sea
so teems with fish, a wonder they didn't
leap into our skiff when we found this haven,
sheltered by a reef from Poseidon's storms.

Fruit's ample as if blessed by Demeter.
Also, high ground, so we can keep a watch
for sea marauders; we'll set deadly snares
and we've the arms I took with us from Troy

So you agree this island's a good home:
a refuge from the scum who slew your man,
Axia; your dear father, Miletes?
And for me, worn out from war, from monsters,
then banished from Ithaca by my son,
this is as good a haven as any
we'll likely find in this perilous world.

Odysseus on the Island

I wake without reaching for a wineskin,
nor dreading the tiny wraith who plagued me,
his eyes sharper than my bronze battle sword
when we burst from the Horse, ten years of war
driving me to slaughter all in my path.

The specter of that child had haunted me
ever since, but he seems at peace, for now,
with my caring for Axia and her son.

We sailed from Troy's graveyard, and found refuge
on this far strand. Miletes and I catch
fish as if plucking grapes, fruits flourish here
like bees; there's barley to grind into bread,
and I've built a hut; our beach free of raiders.

Still, I worry that our Halcyon days
will be upended by men who live
for love of murder. Each dawn and evening,
little Miletes scrambles up a pine
and searches for ships; each time the sea's empty.

But I fear we'll be overrun by men
of violence, men like I used to be,
and must be again, if we are to survive.

On Their Island Refuge, Axia Contemplates Odysseus

Talon lines crease his brow, but he's still spry
as an ibex dashing about Mount Ida,
a sparkle in his eye when he carries home
a boar: dried and cured, good eating for weeks.
He's built our hut with snug stones he carried
back to camp, with my dear Miletes' help.
I smile at his efforts; Odysseus
claps him gently on the back and tousles
his hair to show him, "Well done, my good lad!"

My son needs a father, now that his own
is dead, murdered by marauders, but still
it saddens me to see him start to forget
Melios, though that's the way with the young:
forgetting is how they tamp down the terror
our world's only too glad to heap on them:
as when we watched in horror, as my dear
Melios bled, and those killers dragged me
off, used me as no woman should be used.

Before we sailed to this island haven,
I told Odysseus I'd not share his bed,
the memory and lingering pain, over
what those creatures did to me too savage,
the thought of a man other than Melios
taking me makes me tremble as if Lord
Poseidon has turned dry land to sea waves;

the many-armed-monster Odysseus
told of, crushing me in its tentacles,
defiling me, denying me death's blessing.

Miletes Thinks of His Mother and Odysseus

Mother fears I've forgotten Father. Never!
He talks to me, tells me stories I clap my
hands to hear, but when I try to hold him,
I awake, alone, wipe away my tears,
my heart beating like I'm running a race,
Father cheering me on to victory,
Father, the bravest man in our village,
his sword sending raiders to dark Hades,
until the cowards stabbed him from behind,
then went for Mother like packs of jackals.

I tried to run at them, but they just laughed
and tossed me aside, my head striking the ground.
When I awoke, they were gone; Mother lay
in a pool of blood I tried to stop, but
it oozed, like mountains' red, fiery flows
when Titans try to escape Tartarus.

Somehow I got her into an old skiff
that drifted to Troy's bone-filled battlefield.
There, Odysseus found us, bound Mother's wounds,
told of the War fought there. When Mother healed,
he asked if we wished to accompany him.

I was eager, the man a great fighter,
though no match for Father in a fair fight.

Odysseus Thinks of Axia

Axia, little Miletes, and I've fetched up
on this island, after our chance meeting
on Troy's war ravaged plain. I saved her life
amid the ghosts and bones, and they saved mine,
my heart in turmoil at killing a boy
small as Miletes, the night that Troy fell.

We sailed off and found a safe haven here,
fish all but throwing themselves into nets,
and fruits and vegetables for the plucking,
game practically begging for my arrows,
and grapes burst on my tongue, though I resist
crushing them into wine, once the drink's slave.

All that's missing, Axia lying with me;
but she was so brutally used by raiders,
she made it clear as rain that she wanted
none of the writhing delight of bodies.

So when I saw her walking to the creek—
not in her first youth, but still beautiful—
I didn't follow, not wanting to wake
the horror that still trembles her, to recall
those sea rats who slew her husband, used her,
and tossed her away, like a tattered rag.

I pray to Queen Hera, that Axia
will someday take me under the bear-skin
she made from the beast that gave me its life,
as I'd give mine, to save her and Miletes,
the only family that's left to me
on our glorious island sanctuary.

But best not praise overmuch its beauties,
for fear of waking the wrath of the gods,
who torment those who boast of their happiness.

Axia Thinks Further About Odysseus

I feared he'd sneer, "I saved your life, repay me,"
in the way men most require gratitude.
But he hasn't, though I see his appraising
when he thinks I don't notice, but so far
he respects I'm still grieving my slain husband,
those raiders using, then leaving me for dead,
a matter of the gods' whim that my son
and I fetched up on Troy's death-plain, nothing
but bones and ghost winds—Odysseus
back at Ilium, to try to atone
for the small life he snuffed the night the Greeks
rampaged from the Great Horse, to end that war.

Last night I dreamt of those raiders again,
my breaths a wheezing bellows; then I felt
a rough hand caress and soothe my forehead,
heard whisperings as if to calm a filly
panicked by storms sent by Thunderbolt Zeus.
And there was Odysseus singing softly,
to stop my heart from hammering.
When my breathing was a murmur again,
he started to leave for his own pallet,
but I held his hand, partly to thank him,
partly to ask him to stay beside me:

the three of us—Odysseus, my son
Miletes, and I—sedately spooning,
till sweet, dreamless sleep drifted down on me.

Axia, While Odysseus Takes Her Son Miletes on His First Hunt

Why did I agree? Miletes but ten,
begging, "Please, please!" Odysseus swearing,
"We'll hunt squirrels, fawns, rabbits, not wild boars."

"Like the tusked monster that did that?" I pointed
to his scar that zig-zags from knee to thigh,
and he was bigger, older than my darling,
but Miletes totes his small spear and bow,
strides as confidently as Orion.
Better, had we fetched up on an island
with no wild beasts that attack when cornered.

"Keep him safe," I hiss to Odysseus,
but the old coot fills my dear's head with tales
of the War, Miletes longing to have
won glory there. I tell him glory's but
a brief puff of smoke. A loving wife, children,
a plot of land—that's life. Soon he'll demand
how can he earn them without braving the world
of dreaded men, giants, witches, and monsters.

And how can I answer such hard questions?

Odysseus Takes Miletes on His First Hunt

Finally home from Troy and my wanderings,
I was too god-cursed by the deaths I'd dealt
to be a father to Telemachus.
But I can make up with little Miletes,
and take him on his first hunt, for small game,
I swore to his mother. But a boar crashes
through the underbrush: fiercer than the monster
that ripped my thigh, my first hunt, years older
than Miletes: I shove him behind me;
the beast snorts fire, its snout big as a crater.

When it charges, I let the brute impale
itself on my spear, but he snaps the shaft,
blood flying like a wren in a hawk's talons.
My sword poised, when one arrow, another,
then a third pierce the creature, dead at last.

When I paint blood on Miletes' brow,
his mark of manhood, his legs quake, tremble
at his enormous feat of saving me
and bringing down this monster, his tears big
as ripe grapes, that his murdered father wasn't
alive to witness the deed I will sing,
though his mother will curse me for allowing
Miletes to come that close to danger.

Life, under Zeus' sky is unfair and cruel.
Yet I bless the god for giving me these two
to keep safe until I'm a wraith in Hades.

Odysseus Compares This Hunt with Those When He Was a Young Prince on Ithaca

I still remember my first hunt, Father fearing
it'd be my last: the boar—big as a bull—
charged, gored my thigh; still I slew the brute.
Luckily, Father stopped the bleeding, bound
the wound, had me carried to the palace,
Mother gasping, but all I could think of:
I'd missed the food, the wine, the comradeship
of men trading jests, good stories, and boasts,
while our servants fed us meat and wine sacks,
the first time Father would've let me drink.

Now, Miletes and I hunt out of need.
Still, his mother won't smile at our slain boar,
though the salted meat will last us for weeks.
"No big game," she'd pleaded, "until my boy
has more experience," which meant, "Never!"
But the beast charged us from the underbrush:
Miletes ten, but he fought like Ajax,
firing arrows after my spear shaft snapped
from the boar's charge; the brute finally dead.

His mother will bleed it, after she vents
her rage and terror, for my letting death
stalk the only family she has left.

Indeed, Axia stares, her brow clouding
at the boar, but a look of pleasure, too,
at so much meat, and the blood for pudding;
she'll stitch new clothes, the hide big as a tent.

"And all of it," I smile to see Miletes
grow a foot, "down to your son's bravery."

Odysseus Thinks of Miletes and
His Son Telemachus

When the boar charged, I rammed my spear into
its chest, the shaft snapping; Miletes, only ten,
but what a courageous lad, shot arrows
accurate-deadly as a second, smaller
Philoctetes, our best archer at Troy.

But sadness strikes me like Ajax's fist:
that I'd not loved my own son as strongly
when I returned from War and wandering.
Stupid, but I'd expected a young child,
not a man, impatient to reign alone.
Besides, I was cursed by the ghost of that lad
I'd slain the night of the Great Horse; the wraith
drove me to drink and rampage, so my son
banished me, in the company of two
careless assassins I sent to Hades.

I thought of killing my treacherous get,
but knew I'd be driven chattering mad
as Orestes by the avenging Furies,
if I didn't return to Troy to beseech
the spirit of that boy for forgiveness.

How I wish I'd told Agamemnon's man
to shove up his arse his monarch's summons
for me and my men to sail for Troy's War.

My life on Ithaca was sweet, no need
for glory. Glory? A fucking chimera,
compared to the joys of family, work,
and the serenity I've lately found.

Axia, When Odysseus and Miletes Return from His First Hunt

When I saw that boar balanced on a pole
between them, I stared in rage: they'd ignored
my pleading to hunt only something timid
that will try to escape or feign quick death,
and not charge, the ground thundering beneath
its giant trotters, flames shooting from its snout.

But when I gasped at its rich meat, the bones
for stock, the hide I could stitch into clothes,
the fat I could render into tapers:
I almost smiled. Still, when Miletes ran
to me, to hear me praise his young courage,
I slapped his face for his disobedience,
then grabbed his shoulders that suddenly seemed
so much bigger than just the day before,
and hugged and hugged my boy, out of relief
he was safe, and indeed a little hero.

Or so Odysseus swore, the boar charging
out of nowhere, Odysseus' spear
snapping, the old man praising my boy's arrows,
at first seeming to bounce off its thick hide,
but then, little by little, they sank in,
buried themselves in the brute's vicious heart.

Still, a part of me wished my Miletes
to remain forever a little boy,
my darling jewel to cherish and protect.

Miletes, After His First Hunt

After we slew the boar, Odysseus
dipped a finger in its blood, drew a line
across my forehead, and loudly proclaimed,

"Now, you're a grown man, walk proud!" But Mother
will be furious we didn't pursue
small, safe game; not our fault that boar charged us.
What were we to do, turn cowards, and flee?

Then Odysseus taught me how to clean
and tie the boar to a pole we had to cut,
his spear snapping when the beast charged, its raging
made me jump, but I shot arrow after
arrow; at last, it was quiet and dead.

Like Odysseus said, I'm a man now,
or almost one, once I grow a bit taller
and my voice deepens like the earth's rumbling,
not the squeak of a wheel, like it is now.

The boar hangs upside down, as we lift; my end
sags a little, because I'm not as tall,
though I will be soon, since Odysseus
is not nearly as big a man as Father.

Thinking of him, I wipe away a tear,
my end of the pole slipping to the ground,
Odysseus sees I've been crying, reaches
to grip my shoulder and comforts me with,

"I know you miss your Father, but I'm here,
and together we'll keep your mother safe."

Miletes, from His Island Pine Crow's Nest

Odysseus gave me the vital task
of each dawn, noon, and dusk, to scramble up
a pine, to search for ships of evil men,
like the ones who overran our village,
murdered Father, and left Mother for dead.

Odysseus and us sailed to this island
pretty as the green Meadows of the Blessed,
but when I remember Father, I weep,
though Odysseus is a great hero,
and made me a small sword, spear, and bow
that aims straight and true. We practice each day,
his praise the sun to me, though Mother frowns.

She knows I must learn war skills, but still fears
I'll love these weapons too much, and leave her.
But why would I want to desert Mother
and Odysseus? They love me better
than all the world, and they need me to scan
the sea for ships slicing the waves like swords.

But we're ready: Odysseus and me,
we've built traps in case of a raid; we've dug
ambush holes to leap out and fire darts from;
we've stored weapons, dug pits and sharpened stakes,
in case of an attack. Plus, him and me
are fierce as hounds, as packs of snarling wolves,
and we'll teach those bad men to stay away.

PART FOUR:

SHIPS

Odysseus Sees Ships

From the insignias festooning their sails
and hulls, these two are Polynides'.
He hid rather than sail with me to Troy.
But he's been sent to search if I'm alive.

Telemachus wants him to slaughter me,
and rid my son of the threat I pose
in his fearful head, though I'd never return.
And if Penelope sent that fat bladder
of greed and wine after me, she's hoping,
if I'm still alive, I'll slay him, rid her
of a suitor unwelcome as Troy's fleet.

He's brought too many mariners to fight,
so I'll have to persuade him I've less desire
to return "home" than I would to Hades,
to hear Agamemnon whine forever
about how ill-used he was by his wife
and her lover, when he started our troubles
in the first place, sacrificing his daughter
to ensure our ships a swift wind to Troy.

I'm content with Axia and Miletes.
They healed my soul, so troubled over killing
that boy when I leapt from the Wooden Horse,
I'd have killed myself without their mercy.
Penelope? We were once a matched team,
wisely ruling Ithaca together,

but now, I wish only to be a farmer,
to teach Miletes to be a good man.

I've shooed him and his mother off to hide,
and cached anything that belonged to them.
Now, I await Polynides, with a face
as innocent as Herakles in his crib,
right before the babe strangled two serpents.

Odysseus Prepares for Polynides

Two ships, ten armed oarsmen each; I've set traps
all over the island, hidden weapons,
and sent Axia and Miletes to hide
in a mountain cave, so Polynides
can't dangle them as bait, to force me back
to Ithaca, and collect a fat fee
from my son Telemachus, who, it seems,
now regrets sending me into exile
with the two murderous wharf rats I killed,

though if I were my boy, I'd have done the same
to an old man made loudly, drunkenly mad
by all the dead men I'd sent over Styx,
but most, I'm haunted by the harmless boy
I thoughtlessly slew the night we sacked Troy

Part of me pities Telemachus, champing
like a stallion to rule, but part of me
dreams of revenge on my whelp, though I've no
desire to see Ithaca again, nothing
but a nest of asps. Let me be thought dead.

Well, here's Polynides, with two armed men,
the rest waiting on the strand, my odds better,
if it comes to blood, and I fear it will:
that fat, greedy bastard thinking it's simpler
to kill me quickly and claim I'd vanished
like all the warriors who died at Troy,
than try to drag me back to Ithaca,

when what he really wants is to oust my son,
marry Penelope, and rule as king.

"Polynides, you honor my poor hut
with your esteemed presence," *(you scheming shit)*.

He smiles unctuously as a jug of tainted
olive oil, thinking I'll be easy to kill.

Polynides Meets with Odysseus

I panted up the strand, escorted by
my two best fighters, to protect me
while I'd sway Odysseus to return
to Ithaca, so I could claim the fat
reward Telemachus promised was mine.
That, or have my men kill the wine-soaked loon.

For even old, he's still the craftiest
bastard alive, and could have you believe
the piss he's sold you was an oil-filled urn
then slit your throat like a wheel of soft cheese.

Still, my two fighters are unparalleled,
and I wanted the element of surprise,
so I left my other eighteen oarsmen
with my ships: better for Odysseus
to believe I mean him no harm. So I'll
ask once, with deepest respect, "Sail back home
with me," but if he objects, my men will
kill him so fast he won't know that he's dead
and headed down to Styx without a coin,
while I enjoy the excellence of their bladework.

Besides, unfathomable why he would
prefer this island, bleak as the steppes east
of Troy, when there's Ithaca's treasure chests
so stuffed with gems, my hands would never tire
of fondling them like satiny-moist cunnies.
Plus, there's the greatest prize: Penelope,
who will give my reign legitimacy,

until I can safely get rid of her.

Axia and Miletes Hide in a Cave

"Trust me," this Odysseus assured us,
when we sailed off from the graveyard of Troy,
where my son Miletes and I'd fetched up,
barely escaping the sea marauders
who'd raided our village, left me for dead,
and slayed my darling husband, Melios.

This Odysseus was at Troy as well,
to atone to the ghost-boy who plagued him:
thoughtlessly sword-slashing the tiny child
he could've sidestepped and spared, the moonless
night that the Achaeans took the city,
or so he confessed to me, my son asleep.

"Trust me," he said, after he'd bandaged my wounds,
fed me broth, then stews, and sailed us to find
a home, far enough away to be safe.
But there's no haven that distant, that safe,
in this world of raiders, and the monsters,
cannibals, and witches he told us of.

So when we found an island and after
a few moon waxings and wanings in peace,
he spotted the ships of one of his countrymen—
to fetch him back, he guessed, to Ithaca
or to kill him—he ordered us to hide.

I took a dagger, to put, if it came
to that desperate end, my son beyond
the cruelty men love, then stab myself,
so we can join Melios in Hades.

"I'll protect you," my young boy assures me.
I smile and pat his shoulder, and tell him
he's a worthy son of his valiant father,
but can only hope this Odysseus
is as deadly and trustworthy as he seems.

While Polynides Tries to Convince Odysseus to Return to Ithaca, the Old Warrior Plots

He's brought two men, left the rest by his ships
in the cove. I've no desire to sail back
to Ithaca with this envoy, after
my son tried and failed to have me murdered.
So these three? I'll slay like hens, but the score
by their ships will overwhelm and kill me,
and what will befall my companions then?

Still, those waiting assassins' hearts might fail:
to see my bloody craft, and they'll row home,
in mourning, to tell my traitor-brat
it's best to leave me in peace, though I doubt
Telemachus will listen to reason.

Polynides makes himself comfortable,
awaits the wine of hospitality,
but after rampaging on Ithaca
upon my return from War and wanderings,
I keep no wine; he proffers his goatskin,
and when I smile and shake my head, he shrugs
and pours his vintage down his thirsty maw.

I prepare juicy slabs of pork for them.
Delighted, they partake, their jowls greasy,
while I nibble and stay leopard-alert.

We won't speak until after they've feasted:
a host's obligation of courtesy,
even if I intend to kill them later.

After Sharing a Meal with Polynides, Odysseus Speaks First

Let's be honest, Polynides, my son
regrets banishing me, and wants me back
on Ithaca, to assuage his remorse
for trying to have me killed in exile.
At least that's what he's told you to tell me,
the lad more like me than I'd at first thought.

Assure him there's no need: no avenging
Furies will rip his heart. On this island,
I've found the peace that dodged me like a stallion
refusing to yield to its rider's reins
when I'd returned to Ithaca: always
reminded of the War; the lad I killed
as if a bug when we at last took Troy;
and the monsters that slew all my men
when we were trying to find our way home,
a home that's now anathema to me.

Tell my son, to enjoy his life, as you
should, Polynides. If he wants a sign
to ensure you speak the truth, take this arrow
from my quiver; notice the feathering;
my son will know my unique handiwork.

Take your crews and your ships in the harbor,
and sail safely home; you've done your duty.
My son will recompense you handsomely.

The two assassins he hired won't be claiming
the rest of their fees. Had he only said,
"Go!" I would've, knowing, in my lucid
moments, he was right to lose all patience
with his god-cursed father: no need for killers.

See reason and sail back to Ithaca.
There's no need for further spilling of blood.

Kallanx, One of Polynides' Guards, Around Odysseus' Campfire

Up to me, we'd not have left Ithaca
to search for Odysseus, but my Lord
Polynides hungers for the reward
promised by King Telemachus: regretting
sending his raging father into exile
in the company of two assassins
the graybeard apparently disposed of.

Polynides told us if the codger
puts up a fight, "Kill him in an instant."
Easy for him to say, with his clean hands,
and Odysseus the wiliest man
alive. It wouldn't shock me if he's got
weapons hidden everywhere, and I bet
this camp is boobytrapped, us not able
to tell solid ground from a film of leaves.
Also, wouldn't surprise me if he had
companions waiting for his whistled signal,
finishing us before we know we're dead.

Like I said, up to me we'd have never
disturbed Odysseus. Let the old coot
enjoy the place. I'd rather disappoint
the King, or lie we found no evidence
the geezer's still kicking: than have to battle
this war vet who knows more about fighting
than I'll learn, though I tower over him.

Still we're here, with a deadly job to do,
so let's do it quick, and sail the fuck home.

Rhenon, the Second Guard Accompanying Polynides to the Camp of Odysseus

I say we send the old fuck to Hades
before he opens his trickster mouth.
When the job's done, the King will pay our Lord
a nice fat reward that Kallanx and me
will share in, or just slit his throat for it.
Lucky for us the assassins the King
sent with Odysseus failed at their task.

Kallanx's hand glides to his dagger,
while our Lord Polynides keeps up
a stream of blather, reminiscing on
their boyhoods, praising the virtue and beauty
of his Queen that Odysseus forsook
to subsist alone on this dreary island.

As soon as Polynides gives the signal,
out our knives will flash, blood flying from
the old codger's slashed throat; I'll clean my knife
on his tunic, then piss on his carcass.

Forget the Trojan War; it's a new age,
one for the young, merciless, and cunning:
like fish-dead Odysseus used to be.

Polynides, After Odysseus Refuses to Return to Ithaca

His eyes venomous as asp fangs, he hissed,
"Leave now or I will kill you and your guards,
no matter that the rest of your men waiting
back at the cove, storm my camp and slay me."

I looked hard at the old man, still well-muscled,
still spry as an undefeated gamecock.
After all, he'd slain the two assassins
Telemachus sent with him into exile,
so I knew he'd gut me like a rabbit.

Still, there were three of us around his fire,
my men matchless in hand-to-hand combat.
But even before I could nod the signal,
he slit their throats as if they were fat hens.
Too bad, they were good hands with their blades,
but not as proficient as I thought them.

I fumble for my knife, but he's on me,
his knife at my throat, as he yanks me up,
shoves me to my mercenary-filled ships.

If I can somehow knock him off balance,
my men will overwhelm him and have him
trussed like a capon, my flagship breasting
the waves to Ithaca and my reward.

Or even better, to use the old rogue
as leverage, for me to claim the kingdom,
the young king filled with guilty second thoughts
for trying to have his dear Papa slain.

As He Follows Polynides Back to the Envoy's Ships, Odysseus Sees More Dilemmas

In among his mercenaries, I spot
his young son, the only thing under Zeus's
blue sky the fat bastard pretends to love.

"Call your boy!" I hiss, the lad far braver
than this swine my son sent to fetch me home.
The boy sees my prodding dagger, sees too
the absence of his father's deadly guards.

"Take me instead!" the boy calls. I'd slay him,
and maybe shock his father to sail off
and leave Axia, Miletes, and me
in peace on this island sanctuary.

But more likely, all of his waiting men
will rush me at the greedy pig's command.
And besides, I can't kill someone so young,
harmless, and courageous ever again.

At least Axia and Miletes hide
in a cave up the mountain. Once it's safe
for them to walk to the cove, they'll give me
the death-coin for the hard Ferryman's fare,
atoning, at last, for the boy I killed.

Polynides Makes a Fateful Decision

Odysseus has grabbed my son, at least
the brat I've acknowledged as my own child,
though he bears my second-in-command
a fearfully suspicious resemblance.
Fear for the boy's safety is my excuse
to unleash my men: hounds ripping a boar.
Sons can be replaced, but Telemachus'
reward for his father's return, alive
or dead, exquisite. Of course, he's too much
his father's son to say outright, "Kill him."

But when he confided before I sailed,
"Bring me back proof, one way or another,"
his hint for me to have the scoundrel slain,
who, on Ithaca, ran wild on strong wine
and memories of the lives he'd cut short,
especially that boy he couldn't stop
blubbering over slaying, when the Greeks
burst from the Horse to at last defeat Troy.

Telemachus was too understanding
with the madman, but finally banished him,
although his two assassins were no match
for the wily old fighter. My men are:
as for taking him alive, more trouble
than an arrow or spear, though I'd bargain
the codger for my ruling the kingdom.

And a grand joke to bind Odysseus
to the mast and Siren-taunt him with how
he was once the most cunning Greek, but now
an empty conch the wind pours madly through.

"He's got my son!" I shout to my trained guards.
The old scamp will soon be one less hindrance
between me and Ithaca's splendid throne.

Boreas, Head of Polynides' Men

I grew up rough, Ma and me gleaned harvests,
and I snared small game 'til I was caught poaching.
"Whip him!" Polynides ordered, then made
me his spy and Ma his slut, to keep me
from shoving my blade in his pig-belly.
Years later, when Ma died and he married
Merope, the daughter of a rich man,
he made me his second, to help ensure
I'd keep his guards from grumbling about meager
wages, the Midas-miserly bastard.

But now, with his young son volunteering
as hostage to Odysseus, I fear
Polynides will let the boy be killed
so we'll overwhelm wily Odysseus:
simpler to haul a corpse than try persuasion.

Neseis is too brave to be the son
of that sniveling bag of greed. That honor?
Mine, for the one time Merope and me . . .
before the dear lass died. Poison, I suspect,
Polynides needing me as his guard,
but the oh so sweet girl expendable.

"Attack him! He'll kill my son!" he shrieks now,
as he stands before us, shouting commands.
But Odysseus puts the lad behind him,
to keep him out of the coming assault.

So I do what I should've long ago:
slit our lord's throat, to the cheers of my men.

Neseis spits, then tears fall, for the man
he called, "Father," or for himself, alone
in all the world now. Except, he has me,
his real father. I hug my dear, brave boy.

Neseis, "Son" of the Ambassador Polynides

Father's second-in-command, Boreas,
treats me with more kindness, never taunting
my stammer, my placing last at races,
my clumsiness with swords and battle spears,
my preference to spin tales like a lyred-bard.

Father dragged me with him on this quest for
Odysseus, to "make a man of you."
The joke? He's useless without his hard men;
good only at guzzling rich wine and taking
kitchen wenches now that he's hounded Mother
to death, accusing her of unfaithfulness.
If not for Boreas, who can reduce
most men to pissing themselves with a look,
Father was a meal for any fighter.

The King ordered him to find Odysseus;
we somehow did. But Father—always better
at having men killed than persuading them—
ordered Odysseus slain when I offered
myself as the old rogue's good faith hostage.

I know Boreas is my real father,
Mother told me before she died in pain.
I cried when he killed Polynides just now,
but tears of relief: no more sneering jokes,
no more telling me to pay attention,
when he humiliated underlings.

No more, "Why can't you be like Archilus
or Leonides?" sons of other lords,
boys nasty as scorpions. They relished
tormenting, pummeling us smaller lads,
just as Father did to me, in private.

Well, no more of that; I can breathe at last.

Before Sailing Back to Ithaca,
Boreas Consults with Odysseus

My Lord, forgive our attempt to drag you
back to Ithaca, when you've made a home
on this small island we found by mere chance.
But trust me, your secret haven is safe
with me and my men, with Polynides
gone to the Halls of Death, a greedy man
I served, but loathed, for how he mistreated
his son, who's really mine, but that's too long
a tale, when all you wish to see are our
wolf-ships sailing swiftly from this inlet.

Polynides, I know, wished to use you
to bargain for Ithaca's throne, smirking,
to King Telemachus upon returning,
you in chains, beaten and humiliated,
"Want your father? Then I wear the crown!"

I'll tell Telemachus we found
no trace of you. As for Polynides,
and my sword slashing his throat, I suspect
the King will be relieved to see the end
of his most dangerous rival for the throne.
I'm a much simpler man, and care only
that it's my duty to serve the rightful King.

Besides, it's past time that I got to know
my son, who spent too many years dodging
Polynides' sneers and slaps, Neseis
loving the bard's craft over grubby trade,
the clang of swords, and schemes to become king.

If only I had his gift to spin tales!

Odysseus, After Boreas Sails Back to Ithaca

Boreas is a good, plodding soldier;
he'll never fathom my son's murky mind.
When he swears he could find no trace of me,
sweat will give away his lie; he'll stumble
over how Polynides became a corpse,
returned home for the sacred, cleansing pyre.
So the truth will spill out: grapes overflowing
from a kitchen wench's blue stained apron.

True, my son will rejoice to be rid of
that schemer, Polynides, but he'll not
trust Boreas, knowing he did find me.
Telemachus will have him disappeared,
after prizing loose my last location.

Then my son will come for me, claiming he wants
only to make up for the two decades
that war and wandering kept us apart.
What he really wants? To make sure I'm dead.
Since, as long as I'm not in the Blessed
Isles or being tortured in Tartarus,
he fears I'll return and reclaim my throne.

I'll gather Axia and Miletes;
we'll leave this fair island we'd come to love
for its riches of game, fish, and ripe fruit;

its breezes soft as the palm fronds that cooled
Helen and Paris' ardor after
they'd smoldered and spent, then lay cobra-twined,
while good men died below, for their amusement.

We'll find a safe haven so far inland,
the tribes won't know what my oar is used for—
just as Teiresias foretold from Hades.

From Their Cave Hideout, Axia and Miletes Watch the Ships Depart

They're leaving! We're saved by that tall man's blade!
When we spied those ships, bristling with armed men,
Odysseus told Miletes and me
to hide in this cave, from where we could watch
all that happened in our camp and the shore.

Still, that knife he gave us was meant to end
us quickly, rather than hope for mercy
from hard men, like those raiders who butchered
my husband and destroyed our small village.
I shudder from being used by those brutes,
then beaten, smashed, and kicked, then left for dead.

So I feared the worst, though my small, brave boy
swore he'd protect me, gripped the dagger
Odysseus told him had been Achilles's,
the greatest of the Argive warriors.

But Odysseus is climbing the slope
fast as a young mountain goat: Miletes
and I run to embrace him, crying, laughing,
for joy of being alive and together.
"Are we truly safe now?" I ask, trembling.

"Our only real safety," he says, "to find
a strand so far away, no tales are told
of its greatness or of its sorrows.

And from that landfall, we'll trek far inland,
so even my two-faced son can't find us."

With that, he leads us back to our camp
and starts to store provisions in our skiff.

PART FIVE:

ON ITHACA

On Ithaca, Telemachus Frets

What's delaying scheming Polynides?
He should've found my mad father by now,
and dragged him back here, for me to lavish
a son's love on him; that, or proof the wine-
crazed reprobate's dead; and if he had to
unleash his mercenaries on Father,
that's the price for keeping peace in Ithaca,
and a way past the Furies' wrath for kin killing.

Weeks have passed since I charged Polynides,
and he sailed with two ships, but not a word,
not a sail looming larger, the death-black one
so we can prepare fitting rites for Father,
no more rages disrupting the island.

And Polynides? If he does find Father,
he'll use him to barter for the kingdom.
I'll wager he delays his return home,
to put me off-guard, thus more desperate.

Mother, when she deigns to leave her retreat,
counsels calm. All very easy for her:
the people love her: Father's grieving wife,
innocent of sending him to exile,
while I try to keep the kingdom sailing
a straight course through dangerous rocks and shoals.

Boreas and Young Neseis Report
to King Telemachus

"Boreas, at last!" the king shouted. "Where's
your master, Polynides?" My tongue slow
as dripping pine resin, I finally
confessed, "I slew him when he tried to have
his, my, son Neseis, slain: and make it look
like the handiwork of Odysseus:
Polynides' excuse to attack
your father, who we found, by the gods' luck,
on an island he had no wish to leave."

"True!" Neseis swore. "Boreas saved me
when Polynides would've had me killed,
so he could steal Ithaca from you, Sire."

Queen Penelope laid a calming hand
on her son's arm, and whispered.
Telemachus smiled, and bid us prepare
the pyre. We breathed relief, and I commanded
my men to hew and stack logs, but first, handed
each the back pay Polynides had stolen.

They cheered and tossed his husk on the oil-doused
pyre. As flames ate that sack of greed, my men
sauntered off to a tavern; I could hear
them toasting me as Neseis and I walked
to a stream, to wash off our caked sea-grit.

"Did you notice, Father," Neseis said,
"Odysseus failed to hide some clothing
that belonged to a woman and small boy."

"In truth?" I laughed, "how clever you are.
No wonder he would've slain us, to stay
where he was. Long life to him, and much joy."

What Penelope Whispered to Telemachus

"So Boreas has confessed, forced to kill
Polynides, to keep that fat schemer
from using his son as bait to entice
your father into his ambush. No need
to doubt him; he always speaks the gods' truth,
even if he kept mum that Neseis was his son,
not Polynides', though obvious:
the two are alike as grapes in a clutch.

"You have nothing to fear from Boreas;
he'll serve you as the great hound Argus served
your father, should another Polynides
try to usurp Ithaca. Plus, the mob
will cheer you as a wise and just ruler.
No one respected Polynides. But
because of Boreas, they feared the man.

"Now that Boreas is head of his clan,
you can rest easy: his men will gladly
tend their flocks and herds, and husband their fields.
He'll be delighted to send you his best
sheep, kine, pigs, and vintages, as his lord.
And after you banished Odysseus,
you need a loyal vassal to keep order
in his rich region of the kingdom.

"Your father never failed to heed my words.
I grieve all those lives he stole drove him mad.
Let's pray he finds peace on his small island."

Penelope Thinks of Odysseus

On his island, all alone? Ha! My husband
was never without a woman: first, witch—
Circe; then that goddess-slut Calypso;
last, that chit of a princess, Nausicaa.
So I'm sure there was a woman with him
when my son's envoy stumbled on him.
He just hid her to keep her safe, in case
he had to fight Polynides and his men.

She most likely healed him of his ghost-cursed
ravings with the eager heat of her thighs.
Still, I feel little jealousy: he'll find
an excuse to leave; some last adventure
will Siren him like a cobra's hypnotics.
If she's lucky he won't drag her along,
to face the dangers he can't live without.

Maybe he fathered a child on her, or she
had one already, and he rescued them
from raiders, always wanting to see himself
as a hero of the helpless, as opposed
to the man who slaughtered a little boy
when he and the others burst from the Horse.

He's far too suspicious to think the hunt
for him is over, though, my dear, it is.
He'll run inland, fulfill the prophecy
of Tiresias: to a village where
none knows what the oar he carries is for.

Let him spend his life there, in contentment
and forget his fate is a constant quest.
The gods know he deserves some peace, as do I,
far from the trouble that always hounds him.

PART SIX:

AN OAR FOR ODYSSEUS

Odysseus and His Two Companions
Make Landfall and Start to Trek Inland

We'll take apart this skiff, burn it, scatter
the ashes, so if my son pursues us,
he'll not suspect this is where we fetched up,
to escape his agents, who'd drag me back
to Ithaca, to shower me with love,
or, more likely, make sure I'm dead at last.

Ah, Miletes, you're a resourceful lad,
spearing enough fish for our evening meal,
while we wait through the night by this great fire
that will burn off every trace we were here,
and also keep the howling beasts at bay.

At dawn, we'll march inland, find safety, I hope,
with a tribe that has never heard of me
or the Trojan War that wasted so many.

Axia, that's why I'm bringing an oar:
partly to fend off wolves, lions, and bears,
but more, to know we've reached our journey's end,
as Teiresias foretold from Hades.

The tribe will stare at my oar, wondering:
A winnowing tool? A weapon? Something
that only a holy man can employ
to signal the gods wish to speak through him?

But one look at me, they'll see I'm no priest;
just a rogue good at trickery and schemes,
though I'll know when we meet this tribe, the time
for wiles will be done; time for honest work.

Trekking Inland, Odysseus and His Companions Are Accosted by Thieves

We'd made camp, lit a fire to roast the hare
Miletes snared—the clever lad—then slept.
I should've stood watch, but days of marching
inland had exhausted me. Younger, I'd sit
up all night, telling tales and hawk-alert.

Still, years at Troy and battling sea demons
had taught me never to completely lose
myself in sleep's honeyed oblivion,
so when I heard thieves getting close enough—
smug in their numbers—I sprang like a wolf
and slashed the throats of two of those vile scum.

Another came for me, but Miletes
stabbed his side and I finished the bastard,
then relaxed. But Axia pointed to one
more shifty thief creeping up behind me,
and plunged her blade into him, then collapsed
into tears, overwhelmed by memories.

While dawn turns the sky gray as pigeon wings,
we eat a hasty meal, then march again:
always East, away from the death dark sea,
and towards, towards, we hope, our new home.

Axia, Miletes, and Odysseus Find a Village Haven

The villagers gawk and gasp at the oar
Odysseus has carried ever since
we made landfall and walked for ten days,
my darling son Miletes never once
complaining, through villages we'd hoped might be
a haven, only for some wag to joke,
"Lost your boat?" meaning we had to trek farther
to a place where no one knew what an oar was.

Now in this collection of huts, some draw
back, as if this oar's a deadly weapon,
some reach out to touch it like a rare gem,
and some fall to their knees like supplicants
to be cured of their many afflictions,
mistaking the oar for something holy.

So this is the refuge that blind seer
told Odysseus of, in dim Hades.

Now, the crowd parts to let the headman through,
But just as we fear he'll give the order
to treat us like wolves, not hard-working hounds,
he makes a signal that's meant to tell us,

"You look weary, having walked a long way,"
and all are leading us to a clear stream,
to wash away the dust and grit of our trek,
then to a central fire pit, for a feast.

Oh Melios, my dear husband, if only
you were still alive for this sweet homecoming.
But life does go on, even without you,
and the thought of my being made love to
by Odysseus? No longer dreadful,
after all we've suffered through together.

Odysseus, in an Inland Village

This inland hill-village is journey's end;
no one here knows of me and my great deeds.
Like campfire embers, all so paltry now:
I've gladly traded war's tawdry glory
and Ithaca's endless palace intrigues
for peace of mind and a serene night's sleep,
a full belly, and fellow villagers
who've come to think of me as one of them.

Last, best, I have, if not Axia's love,
then her warm and hearty companionship.
She surprised me when she lay beside me
the night we were welcomed to this village,
and whispered, "So these good folk will believe
we're wed, thus less of a menace to them."

After her little Miletes had drifted
off to sleep, she took my hand, kissed my palm,
and whispered she knew I still remembered
the love I once had for Penelope,
as she still loved the memory of her slain
Melios; afterwards, we lay sweat-sated.

We pull together well, like a matched pair
of cart horses, here where Tiresias
foretold I'd live out the rest of my days.

Tonight, it's my turn to guard the sheep and goats.
Axia will join me. We'll keep watch well,
though not quite as vigilant as this hound
that has lived with the flocks since it was whelped:
a fiercer sentry than any at Troy.

Miletes in the Village

I like it here, this safe hill village bursting
with game for my slingshot or the small bow
Odysseus made for me; I fish too;
best, boys my age for mates. During the day
we take turns guarding the flocks, and sometimes
pretty little Kaila joins me, and we kiss!

We scan the steppes for bad men on horseback.
We've horses too; I'm learning to ride one,
to join the hunts, to take vengeance on raiders.

When Mother, Odysseus, and I first
trekked here, we feared the villagers would kill us,
taking us for spies scouting how to attack.
But when the people saw the oar we carried,
they scratched their heads, so we knew we were home.
The headman greeted us like roving friends
returned from long, perilous adventures.

Mother's afraid I've forgotten Father,
but I think of him every day, though it's
too often that dark dawn when he hid me
and I watched when evil men murdered him
and laughed, then went at Mother, while I shoved
my small fist into my mouth to keep from
screaming, too terrified to rescue her.

When I'm older, I'll trek back to the sea,
build a ship, and find and slay those bastards,
so I'll see Father laughing and happy,
like he was when I was a little boy.

Klax, the Headman of the Steppe Village, Considers Odysseus and His Two Companions

If he'd come to us alone, he'd be dead
before he could get out a lying word,
for we'd have suspected a scout for raiders.
But with a woman and boy, he seemed harmless.
As for his wooden blade, he showed us how
to use it, but such an outlandish tool:
our waters too shallow to sail a craft.

He told us that a great seer he'd met
in the Land of the Dead had prophesized
he'd come to a village where no one knew
what that paddle was, and there he'd live out
his years in peace, after more years of battle
than even the most ferocious warrior
would care to partake of, and then more years
of roving, to come home cursed by his killings.

When he told us he'd wrestled in his youth,
my son, Galanx, our most able athlete,
challenged him to a match; it was over
before my boy knew which god had thrown him.
Odysseus's head may be woven
with gray, but he was wildcat-quick, knew holds
none of us had seen. He helped my boy up,
to the great laughter and wonder of all
gathered to watch; even Galanx amazed.

Odysseus' tales entertain us
on long winter nights, though few of us think
they actually happened. Still, stranger
things have transpired under the gods' blue sky.

Odysseus Lies Dying

Axia holds my hand as I slip down
to the dark land. Here's Miletes too, better
to me than my own son, who banished me
after I'd returned from Troy at long last,
though I should thank Telemachus: without
that exile I'd not have met Axia,
with whom I've lived longer and happier
than my short yoking to Penelope.

On my return, I was no fit husband,
foaming in guilt over the small boy's life
I stole the night of the Horse. I've atoned,
and at last put his young face behind me,
though Axia and Miletes helped too,
so has this inland village we trekked to:
a relief that I was one among many,
my words heeded in council, but no need
to be more crafty than everyone: just
a citizen called upon against raiders,
or to man the buckets when fires broke out,
and of course to guard the flocks against wolves.

Miletes champs to hunt the marauders
who slew his father and left his mother
for dead, before I found them and nursed her.

That madness will devour him; better a small
life well-lived, as Achilles saw, too late,
when I wept with him, in silent Hades.

"My oar," I rasp to Axia, "to row
across Styx if Charon refuses my coin,"
and wheeze a laugh, at my last little joke.

Axia Performs the Funeral Rites for Odysseus

I wish you a safe passage across Styx;
may you recall our happy years together
here in this village where no one knew of
your deeds when we trekked so far inland.

Now, Miletes chafes to leave and avenge
his father, murdered by raiders. As if
my dear son can even recall their faces.

"And what," you soothed, "did killing the suitors
get me? All Ithaca wanted my head,
but too scared of a wine-spewing madman,
so I was banished; I was lucky to find
you and your mother, the three of us happy,
after many dangers, here on these steppes,
as will you be with that Kaila: the whole
village knows what you get up to when you're
supposed to keep the flocks from roving wolves."

Miletes takes my old hand once we'd laid
Odysseus in the ground. "Don't worry,
Mother," he sighs, "Kaila's with child." The years
will teach him the joys of mending a saddle
or feedbag, of sharpening scythes and hoes,

while I play with their bairns, and Kaila stirs
a stew or kneads a loaf, and life goes on,
as it does for us small folk, grateful for
our uneventful years under the one
blur of blue sky Father Zeus grants us.

EPILOGUE

Odysseus Takes His Place in Hades

We sit in silence, the way of the dead
unless one of the living ventures down
and lets us lap blood as if hungry hounds.
Still, our thoughts flow from one to another
like streams set free by Spring's break-up thaw.

In the gloom: Achilles with Patroclus,
and cuckold Menelaus and his fuck
of a brother, Agamemnon, the authors
of our troubles at Troy; when I visited
alive, that venomed asp, Agamemnon,
cursed his wife, Clytemnestra, for his murder,
but the greedy boar slew their own daughter
Iphigenia, for a fair wind to Troy
and its store houses of glittering riches.

As for Menelaus, his face still red
with rage whenever he thinks of Helen.
If she weren't immortal and laughing
at us for saluting her with our peggos
whenever she let her gown slip off her
luscious shoulders, he'd slay her over
and over, for running off with Paris,
whose idea of war was the one in bed.

"Was your long life happy?" Achilles asks.

"I went mad," then stop, too painful to tell,
and wonder if the child I slew is here,
or in Elysium, as he should be.

But Achilles insists I continue:
"We have all of time, here, so tell the tale
with each embellishment you were famed for."
He sits back, hoping for the endless lies
I spun, like the cleverest of spiders.

Even great Ajax, who hates me, draws near.

About the Author

An Oar for Odysseus is Robert Cooperman's swansong to his multi-volume homage to Homer's *The Odyssey,* the first literary love of his life, going back to his junior high school's library, where he found a prose translation and fell instantly in love with the larger-than-life rapscallion and his breathtaking and heart-stopping adventures.

Along with his love for Homer, even if the bard was merely a scribe writing down what had been a long and glorious oral tradition, Cooperman has had a lifelong love affair with the Grateful Dead, about whom he's written extensively, including a mini-*Canterbury Tales* version of the medieval folktale from which the band took their name.

Cooperman has published more than 20 volumes of poetry, most recently, *Steerage* and *The Death and Rebirth of Ophelia,* both from Kelsay Books. *In the Colorado Gold Fever Mountains* won the Colorado Book Award for Poetry, and *Draft Board Blues* (FutureCycle Books) was named one of the Ten Best Books by a Colorado Author by *Westword Magazine* in 2017.

www.ingramcontent.com/pod-product-compliance
Lightning Source LLC
Chambersburg PA
CBHW022138160426
43197CB00009B/1342